3 4028 06898 3072
HARRIS COUNTY PUBLIC LIBRARY

J 597.3 Mar
Markle, Sandra
Sharks : biggest! littlest!

W9-AKC-649 $16.95
                        5123487
1st ed.   02/11/2009

DISCARD

SHARKS

BIGGEST! LITTLEST!

Sandra Markle

Photographs by Doug Perrine

BOYDS MILLS PRESS

HONESDALE, PENNSYLVANIA

Some sharks are big.

This is a Whale Shark.

It's the biggest kind of shark.

Some Whale Sharks are as long as an eighteen-wheel tractor-trailer.

Big or little, sharks have a head, body, and tail. The tail sweeps side to side to move the shark forward. Fins on top and bottom keep it from rolling over. Side fins let it steer.

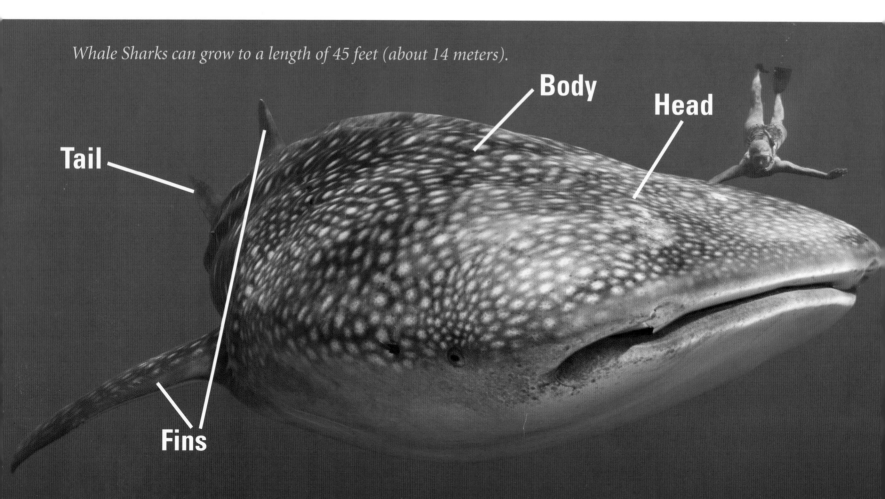

Whale Sharks can grow to a length of 45 feet (about 14 meters).

Body

Head

Tail

Fins

Spined Pygmy Sharks grow to a length of only 10 inches (about 25 centimeters).

Some sharks are little.

This is a Spined Pygmy Shark.

It's one of the littlest kinds of sharks.

Adults grow to be only a little shorter than a sheet of notebook paper.

An adult Basking Shark can be as long as
32 feet (about 10 meters).

So why be big?

For some sharks, being big helps them get enough to eat.

This Basking Shark is another of the world's biggest sharks.

Its large size lets it have a super-big mouth.

Basking Sharks and Whale Sharks eat only little fish and plankton, tiny animals drifting in the water.

These prey are too little for most predators to bother with.

They would be too little for such big sharks, but the sharks can open wide to eat a lot all at once.

These are just some of the hundreds of tiny teeth in a Whale Shark's jaws.

The Whale Shark doesn't use its teeth to catch or even bite its prey, though.

A Whale Shark catches prey another way.

It swims with its big mouth open.

This pushes water through its gills, parts that let oxygen in the water pass into its body. In the gills, rake-like parts also snag the little fish and plankton.

When these rake-like parts become clogged with prey, the shark swallows.

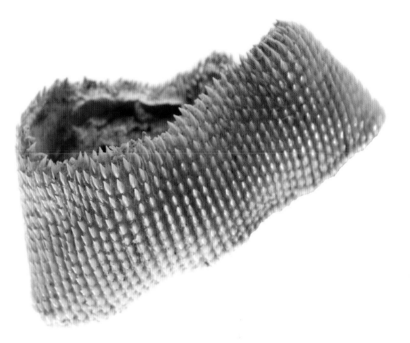

Scientists think having such a big body also lets Whale Sharks and Basking Sharks store lots of food energy. So they can survive when prey is scarce.

A Great White Shark is yet another of the world's biggest kinds of sharks.

In fact, it is one of the biggest hunters in the sea.

So it is able to catch seals and other prey too big for most predators to kill.

A Great White Shark can be 20 feet (6 meters) long.

Great White Sharks use their big teeth to catch their prey.

Each jaw is lined with nearly a hundred razor-sharp teeth.

Its biggest teeth can be 2 inches (5 centimeters) long.

It doesn't matter if biting sometimes knocks out a tooth.

Spare teeth, five or more rows of them, are waiting to move forward, filling any gaps.

Once an even bigger kind of shark, called a Megatooth Shark, lived in the ocean. It was believed to be about the size of a Whale Shark, but it's now extinct, meaning no more are alive. Compare one of its teeth with a tooth from today's Great White Shark.

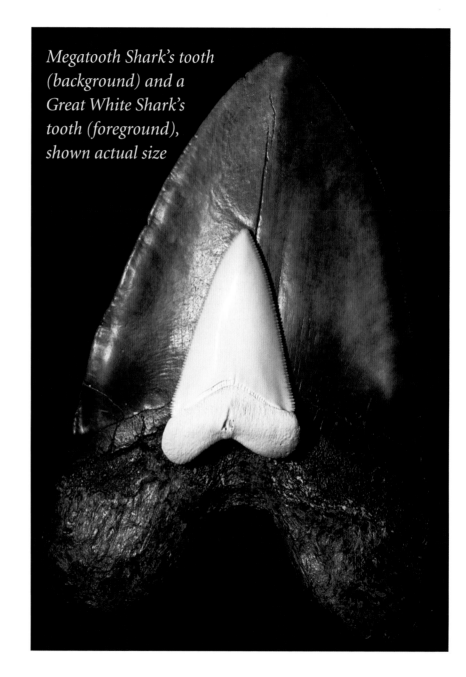

Megatooth Shark's tooth (background) and a Great White Shark's tooth (foreground), shown actual size

For other sharks, like the Cookie-Cutter Shark, being little is the key to survival.

The Cookie-Cutter's size helps it play a trick to gain a meal.

Look at this drawing of a Cookie-Cutter.

Except for a band behind its jaws, its belly is covered with cells that glow.

Seen from below, this shark is so small it does not stand out.

Its glowing body also helps it "disappear" against the bright surface water.

The dark band stands out, though.

This catches the attention of hungry predators swimming past.

The Cookie-Cutter Shark is just 19 inches (about 48 centimeters) long.

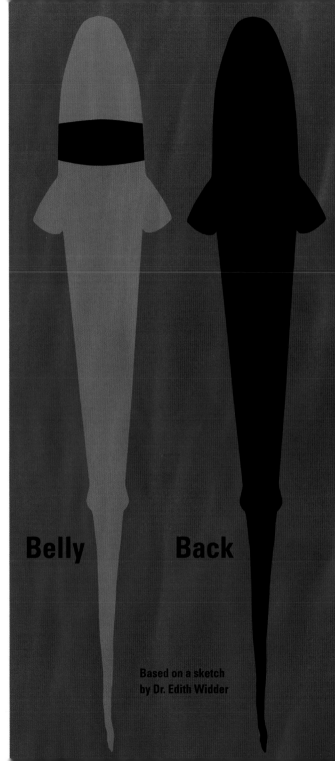

Belly   Back

Based on a sketch
by Dr. Edith Widder

The Cookie-Cutter's eyes are positioned to let the shark look down and keep watch.

When it sees a predator come close, it twists around and bites.

Now the predator is the prey.

The shark's fleshy lips lock on and its long, sharp lower teeth dig in.

The predator's forward motion makes the Cookie-Cutter Shark spin around.

This way, its teeth slice out a cookie-shaped plug of flesh.

Then it lets go and swims away fast.

Being little, this shark can get by on meals too small for bigger predators.

No matter its size, a shark's body is covered with little parts called denticles (DEN-ti-kelz).

They fit together to give a shark a protective armor coat.

Denticles are not overlapping plates, like a bony fish's scales.

They are like little teeth, complete with a soft center pulp and a hard covering of enamel.

Denticles are lost and replaced throughout a shark's life.

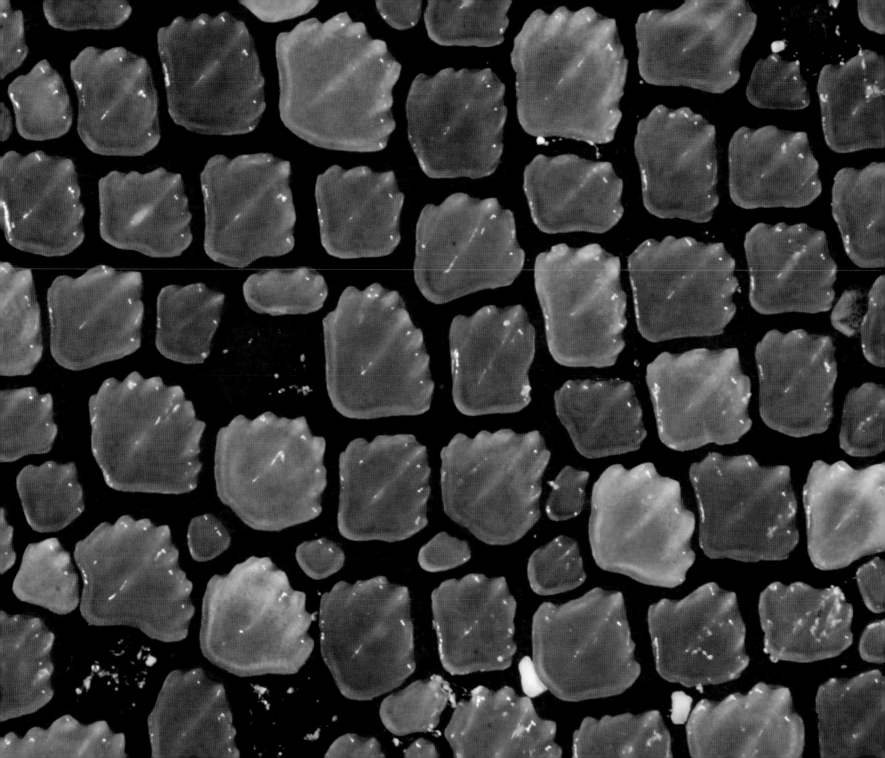

Some sharks have big body parts.

A Thresher Shark has an extra-long tail.

Some kinds of Thresher Sharks grow to be as long as 20 feet (about 6 meters).

Nearly a third of that length is tail.

A Thresher Shark uses its tail like a whip to herd schools of herring and other fish into a tight group.

Next, the shark uses its tail like a club to stun the fish.

Then it gulps down its fill.

The Longnose Sawshark has a long snout lined with teeth.

It uses a pair of whisker-like parts to feel for fish or other animals hiding in the mud or sand on the seafloor.

When the shark finds prey, it swipes its big snout from side to side.

This scares the prey out. And the shark gulps in a meal.

Hammerhead Sharks have big, weird-looking heads.

Scientists believe this head shape may help Hammerheads steer while twisting and turning to chase down fast-swimming prey.

Scientists wonder if having a big head helps a Hammerhead find its prey. This kind of shark has special sensors dotted across its broad head. The sensors detect tiny electrical charges given off when an animal moves.

Some sharks have little body parts that make a big difference.

The skin flaps on an Ornate Wobbegong Shark's head help it ambush prey.

Looking like bits of seaweed, the skin flaps let the shark blend in and hide.

Wiggling these flaps may also attract small fish.

Once prey swims close enough, the shark gulps it in.

The horns (spines) in front of a Port Jackson Horned Shark's two dorsal, or back, fins protect it.

These slow-swimming sharks grow to a length of only about 4 feet (just over 1 meter).

So they could be easy prey for even bigger predators.

However, their horns make them too prickly a mouthful for most to bite.

Horns

A Swell Shark is just a little shorter than
a Port Jackson Horned Shark.

It is also skinny, at least until a predator comes close.

Then the Swell Shark gulps in seawater and swells to
nearly twice its size.

That makes it too fat for some predators to eat.

Swell Sharks grow to a length of only about 3 feet (a little less than 1 meter).

Look at the hatching baby Swell Shark.

Some shark mothers produce just a few big eggs, each enclosed in a protective case.

Then they deposit their eggs on the seafloor and leave.

Inside, the young shark develops while attached to its food source, a yolk ball.

As the baby grows bigger, its food supply shrinks.

It took about nine months for this baby Swell Shark to be ready to hatch.

A Swell Shark's egg is just over 5 inches (13 centimeters) long. Growing until it was curled up, this hatching baby is about 6 inches (15 centimeters) long.

Now look at the baby Lemon Shark being born.

It started life in a little egg that stayed inside its mother's body.

After a few months, the baby shark's yolk ball of food was used up.

Then a special network of blood vessels formed, letting food energy pass to the baby shark from its mother.

That way, the baby shark continued to develop and grow bigger for about a year.

A female Lemon Shark may have seventeen young developing at once. A newborn is about 18 inches (46 centimeters) long. As an adult, it will grow to be as long as 6.5 feet (about 2 meters).

For a baby shark, growing up is all about becoming as big or as little as it was meant to be.

Some are little.

Others, like this Great White, are BIG.

A shark's size is its very life.

That is how each different kind of shark has adapted to survive in its own special part of the world's oceans.

Where in the World Do These Sharks Live?

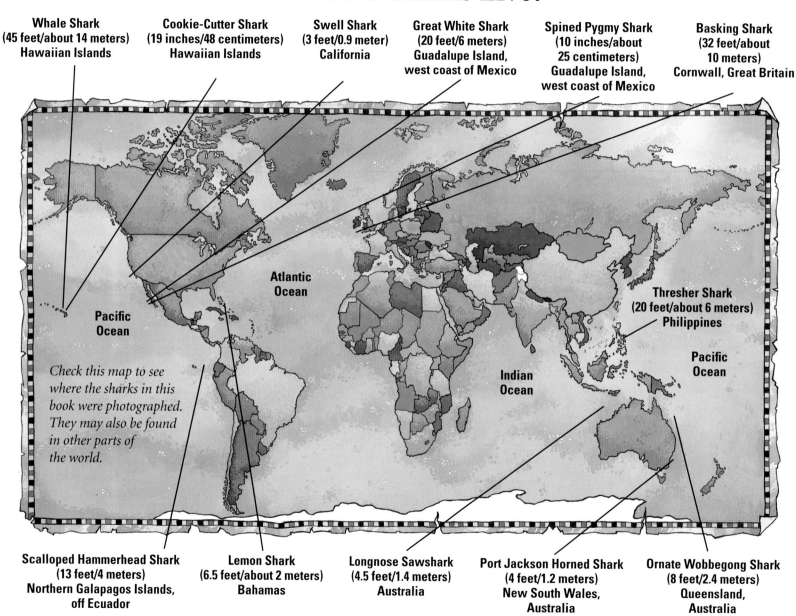

Whale Shark
(45 feet/about 14 meters)
Hawaiian Islands

Cookie-Cutter Shark
(19 inches/48 centimeters)
Hawaiian Islands

Swell Shark
(3 feet/0.9 meter)
California

Great White Shark
(20 feet/6 meters)
Guadalupe Island,
west coast of Mexico

Spined Pygmy Shark
(10 inches/about
25 centimeters)
Guadalupe Island,
west coast of Mexico

Basking Shark
(32 feet/about
10 meters)
Cornwall, Great Britain

Atlantic
Ocean

Pacific
Ocean

*Check this map to see
where the sharks in this
book were photographed.
They may also be found
in other parts of
the world.*

Indian
Ocean

Thresher Shark
(20 feet/about 6 meters)
Philippines

Pacific
Ocean

Scalloped Hammerhead Shark
(13 feet/4 meters)
Northern Galapagos Islands,
off Ecuador

Lemon Shark
(6.5 feet/about 2 meters)
Bahamas

Longnose Sawshark
(4.5 feet/1.4 meters)
Australia

Port Jackson Horned Shark
(4 feet/1.2 meters)
New South Wales,
Australia

Ornate Wobbegong Shark
(8 feet/2.4 meters)
Queensland,
Australia

Shark Words You Learned

Denticles [DEN-ti-kelz] teeth-like parts covering a shark's body.

Egg [eg] the name given to the female reproductive cell; also the name given to the fertilized egg that will produce a baby shark.

Fin [fin] a body part that propels a shark through the water, helps it turn, or keeps it from rolling over.

Gill [gil] a body part that lets a shark obtain oxygen from the water.

Predator [PREH-deh-tor] an animal that catches other animals, its prey, in order to eat and live.

Prey [pray] animals that predators catch and eat.

Yolk [yohk] food supply for developing young.

For More Information

To find out more about sharks, check out the following books and Web sites.

Books

Berger, Melvin, and Gilda Berger. *What Do Sharks Eat for Dinner?* Scholastic Question and Answer Series. New York: Scholastic, 2001.
Explore a world of amazing facts about sharks.

Markle, Sandra. *Outside and Inside Sharks*. New York: Atheneum, 1996.
Find out how a shark's body parts work together to help it survive and produce young.

Simon, Seymour. *Incredible Sharks*. SeeMore Readers Series. New York: SeaStar, 2004.
Learn about shark traits and behavior.

Web Sites*

Aware Kids
www.projectaware.org/kids/html/sharks.asp
Find out why sharks need protecting and what kids can do to help them.

Florida Museum of Natural History
www.flmnh.ufl.edu/fish/education/education.htm
Lots of information about sharks and other fish. Includes games and cool pictures.

Kidzone: Sharks
www.kidzone.ws/sharks/facts1.htm
Screen by screen, this site introduces sharks and their features. There are even peeks at internal parts.

Shark School
www.sdnhm.org/kids/sharks/index.html
Play games and check out cool photos as you learn about sharks.

Ocean Research and Conservation Association
www.oceanrecon.org/research.htm
Explore strange deep-sea life along with the Ocean Research and Conservation Association's Eye-in-the-Sea project. Find out how your school can participate. Don't miss the photo gallery.

*Active at time of publication

For Dr. Edith Widder in appreciation for her research and conservation efforts
—S.M.

Text copyright © 2008 by Sandra Markle
Photographs copyright © 2008 by Doug Perrine
All rights reserved

Boyds Mills Press, Inc.
815 Church Street
Honesdale, Pennsylvania 18431
Printed in China

Library of Congress Cataloging-in-Publication Data

Markle, Sandra.
  Sharks : biggest! littlest! / Sandra Markle ; photographs by
Doug Perrine. — 1st ed.
    p. cm.
  ISBN 978-1-59078-513-3 (hardcover : alk. paper)
  1. Sharks—Juvenile literature. I. Perrine, Doug, ill. II. Title.

  QL638.9.M283 2008
  597.3—dc22

                        2007052629

First edition
The text of this book is set in 18-point Minion.

10 9 8 7 6 5 4 3 2 1

Photo Credits: All photographs are by Doug Perrine except for pages 3 and 10 (Gwen Lowe–SeaPics.com), page 4 (Saul Gonor–SeaPics.com), page 5 (S. Humphreys, Australian Museum), page 9 (Edith Widder), page 11 (Michael S. Nolan–SeaPics.com), page 15 (Marty Snyderman–SeaPics.com), page 22 (David Wrobel–SeaPics.com), page 25 (Mark Conlin–SeaPics.com), and page 29 (Jeff Rotman–SeaPics.com).

Acknowledgments: The author would especially like to thank Dr. Edith Widder, Ocean Research and Conservation Association, and Dr. George H. Burgess, director, Florida Program for Shark Research, University of Florida, for sharing their expertise and enthusiasm. A special thank-you to Skip Jeffery for his help and support throughout the creative process.

Note to Parents and Teachers: The books in the BIGGEST! LITTLEST! series encourage children to explore their world. Young readers are encouraged to wonder. They are guided to discover how animals depend on their special body features to succeed in their particular environments.

"Each plant or animal has different structures that serve different functions in growth, survival, and reproduction. An organism's patterns of behavior are related to the nature of that organism's environment, the availability of food, and the physical characteristics of the environment." —National Science Education Standards as identified by the National Academy of Sciences

Harris County Public Library
Houston, Texas